Watercolor Memories Of The Hills

The Saturday Shop

CLARKESVILLE, GEORGIA

By *John Kollock*

Published by

The Saturday Shop

P.O. Box 307
Clarkesville, GA 30523

Manufactured in the United States
Printed by
Colson Printing Company
Valdosta, Georgia

ISBN 0-9613242-2-8

Second Printing 2005

Dedicated to
the ladies in my life
Margaret, Nancy, Carey, Kathleen, Meg
and others too numerous to mention.

On the Square, Clarkesville

Detail

INTRODUCTION

This is a book of memories. A few of them are mine, but most of them belong to the people who have lived in the towns, villages, and crossroads these pictures have recreated. As an artist, I have always stored images of the world I grew up in, along with the feelings they evoked; as an illustrator, I love to bring these scenes to life; as an historian of sorts, I have come to feel the necessity of preserving the past as accurately as possible so that generations to come might have a better picture of this little world of Northeast Georgia. This is our heritage. It is not grand or earthshaking. What we do have is a tapestry of little glimpses of yesterday that can still touch our hearts.

In 1976, the first edition of *These Gentle Hills* was published. The original book included sixteen pages of watercolor paintings to capture the feeling of the text. In subsequent issues of the book, the color was eliminated in the interest of cost. I have regretted the loss, but understand the necessity of keeping the printing cost down while still having the text and line art available for those interested in learning about our history.

I have been doing watercolors since the early 1960s. The subject matter then was most often based on the existing rural world around me. During those times, there was a wealth of material everywhere. The buildings,

the farms and the life of rural Georgia seemed an endless source of inspiration.

I was brought up short when the old courthouse in Clarkesville was torn down and the surrounding landscape reduced from stately oaks to a few little dogwood trees. It struck me that we had lost not only a landmark but tangible evidence of our heritage that would remain only as a mental image for those who could remember how things had looked. Later generations would not be able to appreciate what had been so much a part of the town for nearly a hundred years.

I decided to remedy this in the only way I was able. Armed with old photographs and my own memories, I set out to bring back the past in a painting. I chose a time when the park in the middle of town was filled with trees. Along one side of the square, the old *Habersham House Hotel* had until 1943 welcomed visitors to its wide rambling porches. The little gasoline trolley that brought visitors from the station into town had once rattled along in front of the courthouse. On the corner across from the courthouse stood the Martin building, dating from 1907. This was the only remaining structure left to act as a focal point for orienting those looking at the painting.

Since I had spent so much time in research, in addition to producing the painting, I determined to do reproductions of the work in order to be able to share the past with a greater audience. That was how this series of historic recreations began.

Of course, I continued to do landscapes and an occasional interior of places that spoke to me. But I began to realize that what I enjoyed most was using my mind's eye to put the world around me back as it had been when I was young. After all, I had been given the opportunity to live in a time which today would be considered a time warp. The decades of the '30s and '40s were not unlike the way our area had been since it was first settled. Then we were a network of little dusty red clay roads. Travel and farm work were still dependent to a large degree on horse and mule power. This was especially evident during the war years when gas was rationed.

Being a small impressionable child, I soaked up everything. I have often felt that I was more an observer of life than I was a part of it – as if I were filling in the pages of a mental sketchbook to be referred to in later years. The memories of the adult conversations I had listened to became my own past as well. These recollections of older people have acted as a bridge back into the world before I came along. It was only natural therefore that as I began to piece together my paintings of yesterday, I sought out firsthand accounts whenever possible to enrich my "*mental palette.*" When I finally began to paint, I felt as if I were back in the time of the painting. I still continually check myself to see that the painting "*present*" is correctly located in the "*historic past.*" The camera can capture an instant of the present; the artist is not that limited.

This book is the result of those efforts which have spanned over twenty years. It is also intended as a companion to *These Gentle Hills*, as visual "*music*" to accompany the "*words*" of the earlier book. I shall try not to keep repeating myself, but let the pictures tell the story. However, in my rambling way, I want to tell at least a little of the background involved in some of the paintings. If I begin to bore you, just skip the words and enjoy the pictures. They say a painting is worth a thousand words – if so, then this is the longest book I have ever written!

My greatest hopes are that this book may bring back warm memories for some who have lived them and that these scenes will help those who are still young, or new members of our community, to value the richness of our past.

Nora Mill

Nora Mill

It was several years after I did the Clarkesville Courthouse that I decided to continue what has become my historic print series. My first choice then was to recreate Nora Mill as it would have looked before the pavement made its way along Highway 75 bound for Unicoi Gap. Nora Mill stands just north of Nacoochee Valley with its backside washed by the Chattahoochee River.

Back in the 1960s, I did an article for *Georgia Magazine* on water mills in our area. At that time, many of them were still grinding corn for their neighbors and the occasional tourists who happened along. By 1984, Nora Mill was almost the last one still operating for its original purpose. Some had become craft shops while others, sadly, had just washed away or "*gone to earth again.*" Nora has kept her wheel turning and enlarging the varieties of products since 1876 when John Martin built his home and operation here. Nora's name came from the sister of Dr. L. G. Hardman, who bought the property in 1905.

My decision to date the prints has forced me to do a great deal more research as to what might be in the picture. Buildings, particularly in a town, evolve and change over the years. Costumes, automobiles, and other details play an important part in giving the setting the right look. Needless to say, my research library has grown over the years, but the fact that I enjoy the search as much as the actual painting time has made each project more exciting for me. In fact, when I finally get down to the painting, I am surrounded by information and eager to bring it all together.

Demorest - 1910

I owe a lot to a photographer named Will Fisher and his daughter, "*Granny*" Harris, in selecting Demorest as the next print. Granny Harris arrived on our porch one afternoon with some of her father's photographic scrapbooks. Will had been the local photographer since the town was created in 1890. Here was a wealth of material to work with, and an eye witness to boot! Later, the ladies of the Demorest Women's Club shared more of Will's handiwork, so before I got down to painting, I knew more about this interesting planned community, created by a group of Northern developers, than I did about my own family history. The view I finally chose to paint is looking north on old Highway 441. The building on the corner is still standing, and the park remains the same. If you look closely, there is a gentleman standing on the corner with an old glass plate camera. This is Will Fisher, who deserves to be in the scene for his help.

For several years, Granny Harris continued to stop by our house when she came from her retirement home in Florida to visit Demorest. She had joined the Army Special Services in her fifties to entertain the troops with a magic show. While we chatted about her father's photographs, she would entertain our girls with sleight-of-hand tricks. They always remembered her as "*the lady with all of those little stuffed rabbits.*"

Nacoochee Valley Road -1925

Nacoochee Valley Road - 1925

Today, when a superhighway bypasses a stretch of former public road, the tendency is to quickly erect signs announcing that the slighted thoroughfare is now *"Historic Old Highway 000"*. I wish that the same had been done on the winding dirt stretch from Nacoochee to Clarkesville so that it would have been preserved. Granted, it was a long slow journey as the road had to visit almost every house along the way, but in its meanderings, it passed a collection of covered bridges, water mills, churches, and old homes that can never be duplicated. The section of road in this painting is coming out of the old village of Nacoochee. The avenue of trees is still standing in the pasture. Dr. Tom Lumsden claims that he is driving the wagon. Could be!

Cleveland - 1912

Cleveland - 1912

Since we had been unsuccessful in saving the courthouse in Clarkesville, I felt the need to praise the town of Cleveland for saving their classic 1860 building. It was also possible in the painting to include the Telford and Kenimer store, the little brick jail, and the Logan-Mauney home on the far hill. I always enjoy the fact that the courthouse was commissioned in 1857 in U.S. currency and paid for in 1860 in Confederate money. One is tempted to wonder what the rate of exchange was at that time.

Cornelia - 1926

Cornelia - 1926

The date of this painting is significant because 1926 was the year when the large red concrete apple was erected near the station to announce to passing travelers that this was indeed the "*Home of the Big Red Apple*". The town was called by several other names, including *Blaine* and *Rabun Gap Junction*, before it finally became Cornelia in honor of Judge Pope Barrow's wife. The Judge was instrumental in getting a building for the station. I had a little difficulty in trying to get the correct appearance of the Commercial Hotel on the hill. Due to several remodeling jobs over the years, I had at my disposal several versions of the front entrance. One photo of the dedication party going up the steps after the apple ceremony settled the matter. No doubt they were rushing in to enjoy the hotel's famous chicken pie which was served 365 days a year. (A good choice, for in the passing years the chicken has become much more important than the apple around here. It is too late to change the statue, however, since Gainesville has already immortalized the feathered wonder in metal.)

Mt. Airy - 1915

Mt. Airy - 1915

One of my reasons for doing historic recreations has been to show how important some areas have been in the past. Imagine the Monterey Hotel standing where the city hall now sits in Mt. Airy. The railroad track was located where Highway 123 runs east of Cornelia. The Monterey had 100 rooms and 50 baths, a ballroom, and its own band to welcome the visitors arriving on one of the many trains each day. Since 1874 when the town was established, this location at the highest point on the railroad from New Orleans to Washington, D.C. had been a favorite vacation spot for those seeking a comfortable mountain getaway. Summer cottages rambled up the hill from the station with views north to the Blue Ridge or south along the sharp drop into the valley toward Athens. Today a few of these homes still can be found here, but the hotel burned in 1925. Even if this had not happened, the days were numbered for resort towns which depended on the railroad. Mt. Airy, like many other towns, lost out to the automobile which could speed restless travelers anywhere a road might lead them.

Sautee Creek Bridge - 1905

Sautee Creek Bridge - 1905

This bridge over Sautee Creek is sometimes mistaken for another bridge which still exists further up the valley. That one actually spans Chickamauga Creek. It has been mercifully spared by having Highway 255 pass upstream on its way to Batesville.

Sautee Bridge was located where Highway 17 crosses Sautee Creek. At that time the road did not run straight but made a sharp left at the far end of the bridge and wound around the hill in the background. The highway department chose to take the shortest distance between two points and eliminated the scenic route around the knoll. The notable sights at the Sautee setting were the water mill and the octagonal office. The mill was commissioned to fill Confederate orders to manufacture hand pikes for use in battle by those luckless Southern soldiers who had no rifles. Governor Joe Brown, who ordered those weapons, apparently imagined the Civil War as something out of the Middle Ages. I understand the order was filled and duly shipped to Augusta, where it remained in storage until the war ended. One of the pikes can be seen at the Cyclorama in Atlanta.

The octagonal office was built of scrap material from a logging operation, hence the use of small bits of lumber which made the shape more economical than a square or rectangular building. It was used as a field office for the farming done in Nacoochee Valley.

Crescent Hill Baptist Church - 1936

Crescent Hill Baptist Church - 1936

It has been hard for me as an artist to leave the beauty found along the Nacoochee Road. Crescent Hill Church is certainly one of the main reasons for my lingering in the area. This tiny Carpenter Gothic building, with its romantic wooden gingerbread details, seems to speak of a gentler time. It was built by Captain Nichols who also constructed the beautiful home around the bend which he named West End. The church was deeded to the trustees of the Presbyterian Church. His daughter, Anna Ruby, was married here in 1885 (yes, he named the falls for her). She moved to Atlanta, and eight years later the Captain also left the valley. In 1898, the Nacoochee Presbyterian congregation was temporarily dissolved. In 1902, a Baptist congregation bought the chapel and renamed it Crescent Hill Baptist Church.

Grace Church - 1858

Grace Church - 1858

I chose to paint Grace Church (now called *Grace-Calvary Episcopal*) in 1858, because that was the period when the congregation was still functioning with most of the founding members. The aftermath of the Civil War scattered the parishioners and reduced the church to a level of poverty which would not be reversed for almost 125 years. Grace was built as a summer church for coastal visitors and a few permanent residents of Clarkesville. The builder was Jarvis Van Buren, whose home is in the background of the painting. *Gloaming Cottage*, as it was called, was surrounded by *Gloaming Nursery* where Van Buren raised prize-winning apples.

The church, which sits on a side street in Clarkesville, is preserved as the oldest unaltered Episcopal Church building in the state. Within its walls there is a feeling of unhurried sanctuary from the world of "*change for the sake of change*" and "*progress*", which usually means dollars in someone's pocket. There! I have gone to preaching just because I am looking at a church picture. Enough said.

Rusharon

Rusharon

This was a commissioned painting for Rush and Sharon Mauney in Cleveland. It is interesting for several reasons. The house was originally in another location and was used by Truett-McConnell College as the first building to accommodate both the classes and dormitory space. This only lasted a year. Later, when the house was destined to be torn down, the Mauneys bought it and had it moved to the present location. In order to move the house, it was necessary to cut the building in half with a chain saw. The final arrangement in this grove of oak trees gives one the immediate sense of the home having been there all the time.

Washington Street - 1909

In creating this picture, I wanted to show Clarkesville toward the end of its time as one of the prime resort towns in these parts. Actually the railroad had already made Tallulah Falls the bigger drawing card. Still, because of the collection of hotels and accommodations Clarkesville continued to be popular, particularly with those who had been coming here for several generations. We are looking down *"Historic Old 441"*, as we now call it, toward the square and courthouse with *The Inn*, one of the popular hotels, faintly seen on the right. In the foreground on the left is the Jackson Home and across from it is *The Charm House*. This was built by W. R. Asbury in 1907 on property purchased from the Presbyterian Church next door. The church had originally faced Jefferson Street, and this land sale made it possible to rotate the building to face Washington Street. The

Washington Street - 1909

trolley ran from the train station to the square bringing visitors into town. The flat car for hauling baggage was called the *White Steamer* since its mule was that color.

I got quite a surprise when this print sold out in two weeks after its release. It seems that the Charm House, which was originally called *Oak Heights*, had been sold in 1936 to become, for a few years, a hospital. As a result, many of our local citizens had been born there and wanted to have a picture of their "*birthing grounds*".

19

Blue Creek Mill - 1925

When I was first directed to this location, I was amazed to find all of the elements of what had been a thriving settlement still in place. This is one of those spots you have to be taken to if you want to find it. The nearest pavement is Highway 255. Regardless of the isolation, it is from just such beginnings that towns have developed; first the mill, then the general store and post office to serve the community. The miller's home is not in the picture, but it was also there so he could oversee the enterprise. Sadly, since I did this painting, most of these buildings have disappeared. The town that might have been, never developed. Perhaps it is just as well, since now nature can at least reclaim part of its own again. That's a kind of *"progress"*, too.

Dahlonega Baptist Church

Dahlonega Baptist Church

This montage was commissioned to show the origins of the Dahlonega Baptist Church and its connection with North Georgia College and the U.S. Mint, built during the gold rush. The group scene recreates the first graduation ceremony from the college. The church is at the left, its bell tower free-standing to the right. In the background is the first Mint building. The present church is the large red building. The stained glass is in the present sanctuary. The gold dome is on the rebuilt Mint, now part of the college. Of course, the creek baptising harks back to the days when that was the way it was done – and still is in some places.

Helen - 1920

Helen came into being in 1913, when the Byrd-Matthews Lumber Company ran a railroad from Gainesville to Robertstown to harvest the virgin forest that covered what is now the Chattahoochee National Forest. It took them only twenty years to destroy the area, after which they sold the mill and the railroad died. During the boom time, the village evolved as you see it. The brick building on the right is still in place; today it has an Alpine tower. The old building housed the Bank of Helen, the post office, drug store and barber shop (which had the only shower in town). Beyond is the general store, and by the river are several buildings referred to as the "*wood hicks' hotels*." The sawyers stayed there on weekends when they came out of the forest. Across the Chattahoochee River stands the mill and the Gainesville & Northwestern Railroad track. Where the public well sits in the painting is White Horse Square. At their peak, the lumber yards stretched the length of the valley below the mill. On the left in the foreground are the steps that led up to the Mitchell Mountain Ranch, which provided accommodations for the executives of the lumber company. The Ranch became a summer resort after the demise of the lumber operation. It burned down in the mid-1940s.

Rabun Home

Rabun Home

In the days before roads were built to get you as quickly as possible to the nearest shopping mall, the small farm was often a self-contained operation. I had determined to paint one that still had most of these elements intact. With the help of friends in Rabun County, I visited the perfect example. There were all of the outbuildings gathered around the homeplace to serve their various functions. It seemed fitting that I should paint it in the twilight, since this was indeed the last afterglow of a time that will never come again.

*Byron Herbert
Reese Homeplace*

Byron Herbert Reece Homeplace

This painting of another self-contained farm was commissioned to honor one of our most famous twentieth century mountain poets, Byron Herbert Reece. Here again, I was lucky enough to find all of the buildings still standing just north of Vogel State Park. With the help of old photographs, I could bring the scene back to the time when Reece still farmed here. The bottom land had gone to broom sedge and pines, but it was easy to visualize everything. There is a special quietness in mountain hollows, where nature seems poised at the edge of the clearing, watching to see when you will give up and let it reclaim the soil you have sweated to bring under your control. Reece, following the plow down the dusty corn rows, found words to express what that life was like. The play, *Reach of Song*, performed each year in the Young Harris area, celebrates his life and poetry.

24

Glen-Ella Springs - 1889

I have only had one occasion to paint a ruin and then watch it be restored to its former glory. For years I had visited an old Victorian resort hotel on Bear Gap Road when I wanted to do a sketch or painting of a crumbling, but impressive, reminder of yesterday. At that time, in the mid 60s, the daughter of Glen and Ella Davidson was still living in part of the old dining room at one end of the building. All of the tiny guest rooms stood empty. The long rambling two-story porch sagged dangerously. After each visit, I felt that I would never see the hotel again. Then, in 1985, Glen-Ella began to shed her cocoon and become a butterfly again under the creative hands of Bobby and Barrie Aycock. Today, Glen-Ella is a rustic, but elegant, bed and breakfast hideaway.

At the time of this painting, the hotel was enjoying part of the fame that was bringing visitors by train to Tallulah Falls. The

Glen-Ella Springs - 1889

resort springs in Virginia had made "*taking the waters*" a popular reason for finding some place where one could take the purge by drinking mineral waters, no matter how bad they smelled or tasted. The Davidsons had such a spring on their farm. They began to take in tourists and build onto the homeplace until it became a hotel. Visitors were met at the train in Turnerville and transported by surrey over the mountain. The springs are still there for the intrepid visitor to discover, but everyone seems to prefer to drink well water.

Mountain City - 1910

Mountain City - 1910

Detail

This painting was the beginning of a series of train station locations along the Tallulah Falls Railroad. Although this was one of the smaller stations, it seemed to be a fitting place to begin the collection with the feeling of mountains and open space. Mountain City had originally been called *Passover* because it marked the location of the Eastern Continental Divide. Streams flowing south of this point drained into the Atlantic Ocean and those going north eventually reached the Gulf.

Little did I know to what lengths the pursuit of the TFRR project would push me in *"turning over rocks"* to come up with all of the information and details needed to complete what I had innocently set out to do.

To begin with, you don't just paint trains – you paint a specific train. It has to have all, or most of, the pipes, screws, wheels, whistles and accessories that will satisfy the train buffs who are ruthless in their examination of your efforts. I had been accustomed to doing my homework on buildings, locations and other details. I had to go much further to keep in the good graces of these authorities. Eventually, I had photographs and dates of all of the engines, but there was much more to watch out for. I have made enough mistakes in the past, which cost me time spent in corrections, or embarrassment if I let them slide by, so today I send any train picture to my friend Rutherford Ellis to critique before I call it finished. Ruddy speaks *"train"* as if he had spent his life in a caboose instead of *"white collar Atlanta"*.

Be that as it may, I still find railroad stations and the part they play in history a good way to tell some of my picture-stories. In the case of the Tallulah Falls Railroad, much of the development of towns and communities along its path came about because of the location of a depot. Cornelia began as a railroad town, as did Demorest and Tallulah Falls. Some locations did not flourish and became only dots on old maps.

I have chosen not to group all of the trains together, but to let them appear as they were released after many research trips, conversations, and corrections.

School (which is how the valley name came to be in Rabun County). Other information also had to be considered. The large wooden gym formerly had a different entrance, and the small building behind the school had to be recreated from old photographs. After many conferences on details, I felt I was ready to recreate the scene.

When I was young and we had cows on our farm, I often got hung up on barbed wire going from place to place. I had the same sensation when I had finished this print, except I was not able to release myself as easily. In order to add some details in the foreground I included some swagging barbed wire fences. (Fencing in those days had a relaxed attitude, with none of the tension which affects the enclosures of today.) The print had hardly been released when a former student informed me that there had never been a fence there in 1943. He had always crossed at that point at dinner time to get a soft drink from the store just out of the picture to the right. Now every time I look at that picture, all I can see is the fence!

Nacoochee School - 1943

I had a lot of help on this commissioned painting. The school is located just above the junction of Highway 17 and Highway 255. The *Sautee Nacoochee Community Center*, which now owns the building, wanted everything accurate for the local historians, many of whom were graduates of the school. I was advised not only on building details, but where the boys played ball, and which trees the girls sat under to admire them. The building on the hill was included because it was the last vestige of the Nacoochee Institute which had operated from 1903 to 1928. Fire had destroyed the school, and it was consolidated with Rabun Gap School to become Rabun Ga.-Nacoochee

Clarkesville - 1912

Clarkesville - 1912

The Clarkesville station stood a mile south of town beside what is now Highway 197. The distance did not affect business because Clarkesville was already a popular resort destination. In earlier days, the stage coach had come right into the center of the village. Now the travelers could make the same connection by boarding a gasoline-powered trolley grandly named the *Clarkesville Railroad Company*; the rolling stock consisted of only one trolley and a flatbed car for baggage, pulled by a mule.

The owners of the hotels in town would listen for the whistle of the train coming into the station and begin to get food and accommodations ready for the surge of travelers due to arrive in 20 minutes or so, depending on cooperation of the trolley.

My favorite story about the *"rapid transit system"* in Clarkesville had to do with a lady who was making her first trip from back in the hills to shop here. She and her baby arrived by train, caught the trolley, and came to town. On the return journey, her tension over this experience of making connections was so great that she was back on the train before she remembered that the baby had been left on the trolley!

Demorest -1900

Demorest- 1900

In this railroad painting of Demorest, I wanted to show the extent of development which resulted from the depot being located here. As I mentioned earlier, a group of New England developers organized the *Demorest Home, Mining, and Improvement Company*, bought up the land, and created the town as a stock investment with the intention of making it attractive to northern manufacturers who might establish mills here. They built Lake Demorest on Hazel Creek, not only for recreation but to emphasize the potential water power available. Their promotional brochures emphasized the fact that the climate was completely safe for northern constitutions.

In the painting, the little stream coming into the lake flowed from the lower end of Spring Park, where annual *Chautauqua Assemblies* were held. Chautauquas were first created in New York state as midsummer festivals of music, dance, cultural lectures, and spiritual revivals. Demorest adopted this event as one of the attractions for tourists whose presence might add to the income of the growing village. Part of the entertainment involved elaborate fireworks displays. There were also mock naval battles staged on the lake between imitation gunboats and a cardboard fortress, complete with fires, explosions, and the sinking of the gunboat as its magazine burst into flames. Tourists flocked to these events, and special excursion trains from Atlanta offered round trip tickets for $1.50 with the promise of returning the visitors to the city by 10:30 p.m. A floating pavilion, boat houses, and a tour boat which meandered the lake added to the summer festivities.

All these promotions were successful in bringing in some industry, including a saddletree factory and a company which built folding bathtubs. However, it was the *J. S. Green Collegiate Institute*, begun in 1897, which kept Demorest growing. In 1903, it was renamed *Piedmont College* and has continued to flourish.

Auraria - 1834

Painting a town which today has nothing left of its original appearance (except the location of the main street) should have been mostly guesswork. However, thanks to the research of Dr. E. Merton Coulter and others, there were good descriptions of the town and the locations of some of the buildings, which made it possible to create an image of the first gold rush town in this country. The main road through town was called the "*Gold Diggers Road*" and ran south to Gainesville. A stagecoach made a tri-weekly run through town. The first name for the town was *Nuckollsville* for Nathaniel Nuckolls who opened the first tavern. A scholarly visitor suggested "*Aureola*", meaning "*shining like gold*" (derived from the Latin word *aurum* for gold) as a more fitting address. This was soon corrupted to "*Auraria.*"

Auraria boomed from 1832, when William Dean built the first cabin here, until 1838. Houses, shops, hotels and taverns sprang up like mushrooms, with the same amount of permanence. When the county seat was established in Dahlonega and the United States Mint was built there, Auraria declined into a quiet village on a side road about six miles south. This pattern of going from "*boom to bust*" was to be repeated in many more roaring mining camps after the gold rush of '49 began.

Lakemont - 1927

Lakemont station in the railroad series might have been a disaster for me in the eyes of the train folk. Things went along happily all the way through the research. The station was located in the tiny village of Lakemont located on Old Highway 441 just north of the turnoff to Lake Rabun. Lamar Alley, whose family store dated back to 1925, helped me find the remains of the track and station location. Fortunately, I had my own pictures of the depot, dating from 1961, when the train was discontinued.

I felt there should be a contrast between the local citizens and the summer visitors arriving for their vacation on Lake Rabun. Hence we have the sporty group of Atlanta vacationers and their convertible. Clothes are always very important to me in dating a picture – as are cars, hair styles, and anything else that might capture the authenticity of the moment.

When the painting was finished, I decided to check with Mr. Alley just in case there was some tiny detail I had missed. (I could still conjure up visions of barbed wire!) After a few moments of quiet appraisal, Mr. Alley said softly, "*You got the train on the wrong track.*" Indeed, it was on the siding instead of the main line. After major surgery, the painting was corrected and the TF rolled into Lakemont with no damage to my credibility. Don't let anyone tell you a watercolor can't be changed!

Est. 1834

1869–1943

1943

AP 1/10

Nacoochee United Methodist Church

Telling the history of a church in a montage gives me the opportunity to illustrate the origin of a bit of our local lore. The first building, located in Nacoochee Valley on Highway 17, was a simple clapboard structure painted white. The paint, however, was significant because very few buildings were painted at that time. As a result, it was often referred to as the "*White Methodist Church*". The name lingered with the second building. However, the present red brick building made it necessary to revert to the official name.

Tallulah Falls - 1905

The town which gave its name to the railroad was not reached by the tracks until 1882. Originally the line had been chartered in 1856 as the *Northwestern Railroad*. However, quite a few years and several owners came and went before it reached the Gorge and came to be called the *Tallulah Falls Railroad*. The village, which was to grow in importance during the next few years, was located south of the bridge now crossing the Gorge at the dam on Highway 441. Since there was no easy way to cross the Tallulah River at that time, none of the hotel

Nacoochee United Methodist Church

development spread north. It did string itself back along the railroad line to a little station at Tallulah Park.

The station in this painting was the first one built. I had the opportunity to talk with the woman who was the daughter of the station master at the time. The family lived on the second floor, and she had been there when cinders caught the roof on fire. Fire was a continual enemy of Tallulah Falls. On a dark, windy night in 1921, the whole main street of the village burned to the ground. In 1936, the Cliff House, seen on the left, also went up in flames.

The scene here was of happier times when the summer band from the hotel came out to welcome the arrivals. The area would be filled with surreys and station wagons waiting to pick up the passengers and baggage and deliver them to their hotels and boarding houses.

Tallulah Falls - 1905

Clarkesville - 1912

Thirteen years after I painted the first view of the Clarkesville Square, I felt the need to show a greater part of the park and nearby buildings, including the one on the right which had been the U. S. Post Office in my early days. Somehow the sense of community which a public park engendered in a small town created a blend of business and social life which I find appealing. I hear a lot today about the good old days not really being good from those who never had the benefit of living back then. As someone who lived in those time I feel this is highly slanted propaganda to defend the obvious faults of today. Of course back then, as they used to say, "*Money was as scarce as hen's teeth*". But if someone needed a helping hand, they usually got it from their neighbors. There was also more time for enjoying simple pleasures.

Families were closer, too. Out of common need, generations worked together to survive and found things in common to bond them. Church was more important, perhaps because without the security of easy money, people found they really needed faith to sustain themselves.

The sad thing, to me, is that the ideas of "*progress*" and "*making more money*" have wiped out so much that was good in our society.

Clayton - 1938

Clayton - 1938

This is a classic view from the memories of those who traveled up old Highway 441 toward Clayton. When you saw this curve in the trestle, you knew that the town was right around the bend. Actually there were 42 wooden trestles along the 58 miles of track from Cornelia to Franklin, N.C. They ranged in length from 29 feet at Joy #2 to 940 feet at Tallulah Falls. The highest was over Panther Creek. The long trestle at Wiley was perhaps the most spectacular to see from the highway. The construction of the Clayton trestle took eighteen months to complete. The train was met at the south end during this time by a Mr. Green with his wagon which took you the rest of the way into town. It was 1900 before the train actually reached Clayton, and 1905 before the station was completed.

The 42 trestles were vital to the life of the Tallulah Falls Railroad. Rotting timbers had to be replaced on a regular basis, and the need for cutting the right of way to prevent fire was constant. By the 1940s, the loss of a single span would have meant the end of the railroad.

Cornelia - 1942

Cornelia - 1942

Since Cornelia had been the first station on the Tallulah Falls Railroad line, I decided to show it this time in the last burst of its popularity, brought on by the war years. By 1942, gas rationing had dictated that automobile transportation could be used only in cases of need. Those with an *A card* could get enough fuel to carry on needed services. The rest of us saved up our coupons to get where we absolutely had to go. Fortunately the horse and mule were still part of the rural scene, so we simply reverted to devoting a whole day for travel by wagon to shop in the village.

Suddenly the railroad became a people mover again. Salesmen, service personnel, vacationers, and in the case of this picture, the summer campers, all rushed to climb aboard the iron horse. Extra cars were added to supply the demand during the summer. Of course there was no air conditioning. You could swelter in the heat or open the windows and wind up chewing cinders. Regardless of this, there was the never-to-be-

Baptist Church Hill

forgotten thrill of rocking and rattling through the foothills with the black smoke swirling in the wind, and the shrill whistle echoing off the mountain sides as you approached a station. It was the swan song of the Tallulah Falls as a passenger line; the end of the war put the public back in the driver seat. Only mail and freight still got on board. In 1961, the train itself followed the stagecoach into yesterday.

Baptist Church Hill

This is another *"then and now"* montage, showing both buildings sitting on the same spot above Cleveland overlooking the mountains. It is interesting to speculate what activities took place in the second and third story little box rooms of the old building. That is part of the charm of old Victorian design – sometimes you just added something because it struck your fancy and figured maybe later you could find a use for it.

Main Street Toccoa - early 1900s

Main Street, Toccoa - early 1900s

Toccoa was originally called *Dry Pond*, because at the crossroads there was a watering spot in the wet season that dried up in summer. Local legend has it that the land here was of so little value it had once been sold for a cowbell. When the railroad from Atlanta to Greenville was built, a station was put here. As with Demorest and other locations, developers immediately seized the opportunity to buy up the land and create a city. By 1874, Dry Pond became *Toccoa City*. The main street paralleled the tracks and business thrived. Much later this same street was converted to a shopping mall, and the old buildings disappeared behind a modern facelift. In recreating the earlier scene, I used old photographs and did a bit of on-site peeking behind the twentieth century "*slipcovers*" to find the color of the brick work and window details. The various types of vehicles in the picture came from a large collection of photographs belonging to the historical archives of the city.

Turnerville - 1920

Turnerville, or *Turner's Point*, was one of those towns that might have grown, but the close competition of Tallulah Falls made it impossible. It was a little too far south on what is now Highway 441 to compete. Not that it didn't try. A model town was laid out around the station. The large *Wilson Lodge* was erected along East Railroad Street to be followed by the *Fodrel House* and the *Anderson House*. The surrey from Glen-Ella Springs Hotel met the train here, and I was told by one of my authorities that Margaret Mitchell came down the steps from the platform on one occasion. Where she was staying was not revealed to me.

My research was slow in coming together on Turnerville. Finally a few snapshots turned up. My problem then was in piecing together the isolated views. The general store in particular proved to be a problem. I had only one photo of the front of the building – head on. I consulted the lady whose family had owned the building. She had moved to Clayton by then, and the store had been torn down. I can only talk with a pencil in my hand, so using bits of scratch paper and the back of deposit slips to sketch on, I attempted to locate the position of all of the details. After much doodling and discussion, we seemed to be of one mind. I went back to the studio and began the painting. A few weeks later I took the results for her blessing. Now that she could see a painting and not just my doodles, she remembered that the store faced the side road instead of the tracks. In this case I was not as lucky as with Lakemont. It is impossible to correct a painting when part of the mistake extends into a watercolor sky. *Turnerville #2* finally passed inspection.

Departure of the Blue Ridge Rifles - July 1861

Departure of the Blue Ridge Rifles (July 1861)

The use of the Dahlonega Court House in a painting called for a choice of dramatic moments. The building had been in existence since 1836. Its first big moment came when Dr. Matthew Stephenson stood on the balcony and pled with the miners not to go west to the new gold fields. "*There's still gold in these hills*", or something to that effect, was the message. Needless to say, most of the listeners were already scooping up shovels full of gold nuggets in their minds. And their minds were in California.

The second choice was the departure of the newly formed company of volunteers to join the Confederacy in defense of their homes and loved ones. I chose the second option.

Here are the boys in their butternut uniforms receiving the flag from Miss Ida Hamilton, the sister of Joseph H. Hamilton, who had been elected captain over the company. Private W. H. McAfee is receiving the homemade flag which is based on a design adopted by the Provisional Congress March 4, 1861. (Actually there were so many

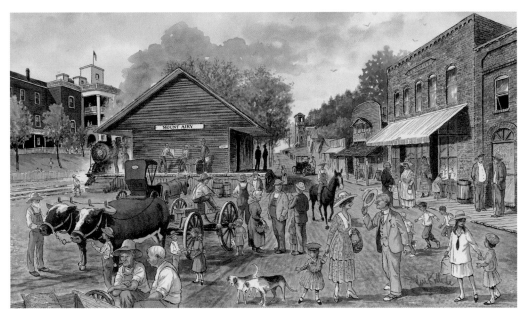

Mt. Airy - 1920

versions of the flag during the war, it is surprising that the troops knew which one to "*rally round*.") In the background is the *Eagle Tavern*, and on the far hill is the first U. S. Mint building.

One other detail which concerned me was whether the men had their own weapons at the time or if they were issued later. Some might have brought their own and others just turned out with only their blanket rolls and anticipation. I was unable to find a satisfactory answer at the time, so I just left the detail lost in the mists of time and fuzzy watercolor.

Mt. Airy - 1920

Mt. Airy is pictured here at the time when business was good and the railroad was serving as a commuter service for gentlemen working in the city while their families enjoyed the summer cool of the mountains. Along the one business street were the *Bank of Mt. Airy, McConnell's Store*, and the center of village life, *Kimsey's Store*, where you could find groceries, dry goods, coffins, the post office, the town's only telephone, and "*coconut cornbread-shaped candy*." If you want to locate this spot today, look for the town well which stood at the far end of the station. In place of the depot, there now resides a red caboose, in memory of those golden days.

Currahee Mountain -1873

Currahee Mountain - 1873

Currahee Mountain was one of the destinations for early visitors to Northeast Georgia in the 1840s. Together with Toccoa Falls, it was a *"must see"* location. At an elevation of 900 feet, it was the last significant mountain before the land fell away into the relatively flat plain of South Carolina. When the first land grant was made here in 1775, the area bordered on the edge of the Cherokee Territory, and several forts were built as places of refuge in case of trouble. *Fort Box* stood where the residence stands in this picture. There are many other events associated with the area. Part of the mountain was involved in the *Four Mile Purchase* in 1804; during the Indian Wars, Andrew Jackson fought a battle at Fort Hill nearby; and the first post office was established here in 1836. There are stories of caves on the mountain where gold was hidden and Civil War deserters took refuge from Governor Brown's militia.

My favorite true story is about Jane Ann Davis, the daughter of Young Davis, for whom the settlement was first named. Jane Ann was the postmistress and lived in the family home seen in the painting. At the far end of the group of little outbuildings was the post office. When anyone wanted service, they let out a whoop, and Jane Ann had to trudge down to sell a stamp or hand over the mail. Around this time, Toccoa City had begun to rise out of Dry Pond. One day Jane Ann just got fed up with her job – loaded the whole post office in the family wagon – drove to Toccoa and dumped the official trappings and the job on the city's postmaster. She thereby physically ended the postal station at Currahee Mountain.

Sautee Store - 1934

I doubt that many people who visit the Sautee-Nacoochee area fail to spend at least a few minutes in the Sautee Store. Mervin and Astrid Fried have made this location a combination country store museum, Scandinavian import shop, and welcome-back-to-the-valley stopping point. Of course, crossroad stores were located every few miles in the days when roads were bad and walking was good. This particular operation came about when R. A. Williams suffered from sunstroke while farming. His brother-in-law, J. L. Johnson, built him a place of business in the shade of some old oak trees so he could earn a living storekeeping. Business was good. The post office opened here in 1893. Other persons continued to operate the store after Mr. Johnson's time.

Sautee Store -1934

In 1964, the post office moved out. The storekeeper let the Friends use the tiny office area to sell imported gifts. That business got so good that the storekeeper moved across the street (too many tourists were interrupting the leisurely visiting of homefolks on the porch). The store was turned into a museum and the rest is history.

One other point of interest is the totem pole in front of the store seen in the background. This was carved by a gentleman called *"the woodcarver of Sautee"*. It depicted the legends of the valley. A fragment can be seen in the museum operated by the *Sautee-Nacoochee Community Association*, located in nearby Sautee Valley.

Baldwin - 1921

Baldwin - 1921

Baldwin's original name was *Stonepile*, because of a mound of rocks once located beyond the public well, at the intersection of old Highway 441 and the street coming toward us in the painting. The street would have been an old Indian footpath coming up from Wofford Creek.

Baldwin was established in 1896 and rechristened with the maiden name of W. A. Willingham's wife. Mr. Willingham was a conductor on the *Atlanta-Charlotte Airline Railroad*. Again we have a railroad-made town. The old rambling hotel was owned by J. S. Jackson, who also built the first brick house in town. The white building in the background was the bank owned by W. A. Shore. This same gentleman can be seen raising dust in his new motor car. Thanks to a carefully preserved photograph of the event, I was able to include this detail in the painting.

Sautee Valley Spring

Sautee Valley Spring

This painting was commissioned by the *Sautee-Nacoochee Community Association* as a fund raiser. The challenge I set myself was to capture the whole feeling of a valley which is usually seen only in little vistas. As it turned out, there is literally no vantage point from which such a view can be seen unless you are ballooning, or hovering in a helicopter over the fire department. I tried climbing their training tower, but soon found out why I am not qualified to be a fireman. I went up on the hill at Sautee Inn and saw mostly trees. At one point, the presidents of the *Community Center* and *Standard Telephone* boosted me up a tall oak in the valley to take a photograph. I got lots of leaves and limbs in my viewfinder. Finally I used an aerial map, a lot of piecemeal photographs, and a fertile imagination to hover, paper and paintbrush in hand, over this beautiful location. The building in the background is the *Nacoochee Presbyterian Church*.

Plowing Time

Plowing Time

Autumn of Burton

When I used to drive regularly from Gainesville to Nacoochee Valley, this view was my favorite of Yonah Mountain. It was just a few miles north of Cleveland. "*Was*" is the operative word in this case. The farm and barn still existed then. By 1993, when I did the painting, the barn was gone and no one was tending the field. Then the tornado of 1994 swept through the area, destroying the house and much of the landscape. So I was glad I could preserve this moment as I still like to remember it.

Autumn on Burton

Each of the lakes in the chain that was formed from damming the Tallulah River has its own special feeling. Burton to me has majesty. It sweeps its way amid the mountains, a broad highway of clear blue water with Charlie Mountain standing out like a lighthouse as you motor north toward the headwaters of the river. Autumn is a good time to enjoy the lake after the busy season of summer vacationers. There are times at sunset when you are the only living being on the water. At such a moment, you can feel as if all of this – water, mountains and sky – belong to you alone. If I may be allowed a contradiction in terms, one feels a sense of powerful humility.

Toccoa Falls - 1908

Toccoa Falls - 1908

Toccoa Falls College began in this old building built in 1899 by Mr. E. P. Simpson as a resort hotel. He called it the *Toccoa Falls Inn* and later *Haddock Inn*. The building had 62 rooms and a veranda 750 feet long. Simpson also built a hydroelectric plant to supply electricity to the hotel and the city of Toccoa. The small building seen across the lake was the power plant. It is still there, as is the lake

in the picture. In 1911, the building was sold to Dr. R. A. Forrest for a Christian college. The school thrived. Then, in 1913 the building burned down, and a tent city replaced the school. Classes continued under canvas for three years as the college slowly began to construct new buildings. Many of the students helped in this work. There were other setbacks, including the tragic flood in

1977 caused by a dam failing above the falls. Still the spirit of Toccoa Falls College has remained strong and the school continues to grow.

The falls have been a scenic attraction since the first settlers came into the area. The water plunges over a shelf of rock and falls 186 feet to the base of the cliff. This makes Toccoa Falls 29 feet higher than Niagara.

Leaf - 1926

Leaf - 1926

"*Where is Leaf?*" That sort of question, which I heard many times while I was doing the art work for this picture, should have put me off of the idea that this would ever be a successful print. However, the combination of a cotton gin, a rural school and a church made me decide to risk working on the research necessary to bring the picture together. As it turned out, the background material came easily from old family photos offered by people who still lived in the area. Also, there were many memories connected with the activities that took place at this crossroads. The final painting seemed to make a lot of people happy.

Leaf, by the way, is still there at the intersection of Highway 115 and Highway 384. It now has a stop light, too!

Watts Mill - 1930

Watts Mill - 1930

There have been two mill buildings at this site on Highway 197 a few miles below Batesville. The first was built by Bryant Hill in the 1850s. The house at the left was his home where he raised 13 children. The road between the mill and the house was the old road to the town of Burton. Mr. Hill used the water power to generate electricity in addition to grinding corn. He sold power to his near neighbors. After his death in 1889, the mill was run by his descendants until it was sold in 1929 to Allen Watts and his son, Robert. By 1930, *Hill's Mill* was called *Watts' Mill*. In 1930, a new building was erected on the rock outcropping, and *Grandpa Watts' Water Ground Meal Mill* became an institution on the Soquee River. A devastating flood ended the milling operation and almost wiped out the building in the 1960s. In 1968, John and Glen LaRowe propped up the remains and started making pottery. *The Mark of the Potter* came into being.

Creek baptizing have been a part of the scene since the early days, although today one is more likely to see tourists feeding the pet trout that live under the falls.

Battle of the Narrows - 1864

The facts concerning this skirmish are limited, but as it was our only regional claim to any real action during the Civil War, I felt I should make an effort to bring it to life. Aside from a few sentences on a historic marker in Banks County, the details were slim. Even the archives in Atlanta confirmed little beyond the fact that the event did take place. Related records of the time gave me some answers.

After the Battle of Atlanta, small raiding parties of Union cavalry, under the command of Kenner Garrard, were sent into the hills to burn crops and generally demoralize the Southern patriots. At a point where two ridges are connected by a narrow road across a steep incline, Confederate soldiers (probably part of the Georgia Guard who had been sent home from Atlanta to gather in their crops) met and defeated the marauding troops. The Narrows is a sort of causeway between two ridges where a band of foot soldiers could have stood off cavalry at a point where horses would have been unable to maneuver. The location is deep in the *Lake Russell Wildlife Management Area*. The road still exists as it was at the time of the battle – October 12, 1864.

Mt. Airy School - 1938

This painting was a commission for fund raising to restore the old building. The school operated from 1922 to 1955. During its short existence, many innovations reached the community and the building. Electricity was added in 1923 and inside water fountains were installed in 1946, but plumbing was not put in until 1951. Early students laughingly remember the little path out back leading to the outhouses which were used in sunshine, rain and snow. The auditorium on the second floor was often pressed into service for social affairs in the community and traveling shows from the *Grand Old Opry*. The home economics room was used in the mid-20s for adult education sponsored by *Athens Business College*.

Nacoochee - Cherokee Days

In some cases, I find it interesting to do a series on the various stages of history which have taken place in the same location. Such a spot is the west end of Nacoochee Valley, where the little Indian mound rises so distinctly out of the pasture wearing a Victorian summer house on its head. The mound, with Yonah Mountain in the background, forms my setting to reconstruct several significant periods in our past.

The time of the Cherokee in the valley followed the age of the *Mound Builders* who formed the first raised earth platform in times before recorded history. The mound was considerably larger than it is today. The Cherokee built their council house at the top with the entrance facing east toward the rising sun. From this location, the village spread across the valley. The Chattahoochee River wrapped around the

setting and was important not only for water and fishing but as part of the religious rituals of the tribe. Excavations made in 1915 revealed evidence of a long period of burials and rebuilding of the council house. Only half of the mound was exposed that year. It was planned that in 1916 there would be more excavation, but the owner of the property refused permission. The activity interfered with his corn crop.

Nacoochee - 1832

Nacoochee - 1832

Nacoochee became part of the expansion of the European settlers after the *Treaty of 1818* with the Cherokee Nation. The treaty was only one of many maneuvers to remove the Indians from their land and ultimately drive them west in 1838 on the "*Trail of Tears*." In 1822, two wagon trains left Burke and Rutherford Counties in North Carolina with 61 families heading to the valley. These became the first families of Nacoochee. They traveled along a narrow road called the *Unicoi Turnpike*, which had been built by developers under an agreement with the Cherokee in 1813. The road ran from the Tugaloo River up through Unicoi Gap and into Tennessee. This was the first vehicular passage built across Northeast Georgia. Today, many of the families in the area can trace their ancestors to this first migration.

Nacoochee- 1923

Nacoochee - 1923

A hundred years after the first settlers arrived in the valley, many things had changed. Following the Civil War, Captain J. H. Nichols built a large mansion on a rock outcropping which overlooked the old Indian mound. On top of the mound, he placed a summer house to admire from his front porch, or, alternatively, so he could sit in the summer house and admire his home. The next owner of the property was Dr. L. G. Hardman, who added the brick store near the covered bridge over the Chattahoochee River. In 1913, the Byrd-Matthews Company established a large lumber mill a few miles beyond Nacoochee and built a railroad from Gainesville to carry their product to market. The mill village was named Helen in honor of the mill owner's daughter. The train served to bring summer visitors to the area, but the main purpose was for transporting lumber. When the mill closed in the early 1930s, the railroad closed down, too.

Nacoochee - 1940

Nacoochee - 1940

By 1940, Nacoochee Valley had returned to being a quiet backwater of farming activities with a scattering of summer visitors who returned each year to enjoy the peace of rural life. There were few paved roads and an abundance of covered bridges to decorate the landscape.

For many people, the land in Nacoochee and Sautee is sacred. For the Cherokee, it is the resting ground of their ancestors. For the descendants of the original settlers, it is a place that holds memories of times when life held hope for a world as permanent as the hills themselves.

Now these valleys have been designated an official Historic District. In this, there is hope for the future, if wisdom can overcome greed. The mound of the Cherokee was ultimately saved by the addition of a summer house. I find this significant. It combines in two cultures a monument to what is important to preserve.

The Crossroad Store - 1935

The Crossroad Store - 1935

It would be impossible for me to count all of the requests I received over the years to paint E. B. Hunt's old store building which stands on Post Road near Cleveland. It seems that it was a fond memory, not only of those who lived within walking distance of it, but also passersbys who looked upon the location as a landmark. I finally decided to paint it in the evening at the end of a working day, when night would soon envelop the scene in darkness. As the twilight would soon fade so would the era of these rural entrepreneurs.

Consolidated Gold Mine - 1904

Consolidated Gold Mine - 1904

When I first went down to see the newly opened tunnels of the *Consolidated Gold Mine* near Dahlonega, I was met with an amazing sight. Visitors follow a winding descent into the heart of the mountain, arriving eventually in a long tunnel with other passages disappearing in several directions like a rabbit warren. Above me rose a huge excavation with a brilliant shaft of light dropping down on the dusty floor of the tunnel. This is called the "*Glory Hole.*" I knew at once that I wanted to capture the scene.

In mining, a horizontal cut along a vein of gold is called a "*drift.*" A vertical cut is called a "*slope.*" The Glory Hole "*slope*" extended from the floor of the mine tunnel up through the heart of the mountain to the very top.

When it was constructed, the Consolidated Gold Mine was regarded as the most ambitious such venture east of the Mississippi. It was organized in 1898, began operation in 1900, and went bankrupt in 1906. Since that time it has stood idle, eventually filling with over 4,000 tons of silt and mud.

Today the mine has been reopened, not for gold, but for visitors to experience what it feels like to go 70 feet deep into a mountain, and walk along the same dark tunnels that once rang with the sounds of drilling and explosions. Here you will find rail tracks and mine carts, mining tools, and the drilling machine powered by air and water which raised a fine dust, causing many workers to die of lung disease. The drill was aptly named "*the widow maker.*"

This massive restoration was done by Bryan and Donna Whitfield, who devoted several years to bringing this bit of history back to life.

Bethlehem Baptist Church - 1925

Bethlehem Baptist Church - 1925

Bethlehem Baptist Church was constituted in 1818, at which time the area had just been taken by treaty from the Cherokee Nation. The church was first located about five miles north of Clarkesville. Shortly thereafter, it was relocated at the present site on Highway 197. The Unicoi Turnpike ran past the entrance, making travel to church more convenient in a time when roads were almost nonexistent. The original building shown in the painting was used, with some remodeling, until 1971 when a large new church was erected.

The location of the older building was across the road from the present church. In the old graveyard, you can still recognize one of the grave sites in the painting. It is surrounded by an iron fence.

Blairsville, Georgia - 1930

The Union County Courthouse was built in 1899 to replace an older structure which had burned. It reflects a style of architecture found in many public buildings of the time, including the old courthouse in Clarkesville. The cost of construction was $12,000, with most of the materials and labor coming from Union County. The red bricks were hand-molded in the area. In 1970, the court facilities were moved to a more modern structure, and the old landmark became the home of the *Union County Historical Society*.

In putting together the details of the scene from 1930, I had to use mostly old photographs and personal remembrances as most of the wooden hotels that stood around the square have disappeared. The courthouse still stands, so I felt that much could be done from first hand observation. However, in looking at the older pictures, I discovered that the bell tower had been removed. Careless of me to have missed it! I found on questioning that the load of the tower on the roof had been so great that it had been removed, rather than have it come crashing through into the courtroom on the second floor.

Tallulah Falls
Land of Legends

Tallulah Falls - Land of Legends

The gorge and falls at Tallulah are a dramatic contrast to most of Northeast Georgia. Ours is a land of gentle rolling mountains worn down over the ages. Our ridges predate the dramatic peaks of the West by many centuries. The charm of the area is in the intimate nature of the woods and streams, the flowers and ferns that blanket the forest floor, and the blue haze that shrouds the landscape most of the year. Therefore, Tallulah Gorge comes as a surprise to those who reach its rim for the first time and witness the abrupt plunge into a world of crags and waterfalls many hundreds of feet below.

No doubt the Cherokee Indians had the same reaction during the time when this land belonged to them. In addition, there was mixed fear and superstitions in their reactions. The roaring waterfalls and perpetual mist that hung over the area gave rise to legends of spirit people who might lure the careless traveler into their caves.

Tallulah was actually a village further up the river. It was called *Talulu* for the *Dulusi frog* whose cry sounded like "*talulu*." The gorge with its terrifying roar was called *Ugunyi*. For their part, the Cherokee gave the area a wide berth and never hunted or fished in its depths.

Tallulah Falls - 1820
Hunters and Hermits

Tallulah Falls - 1820
Hunters and Hermits

As with other areas which have more than one phase in their history, I chose to show several periods of civilization at Tallulah Falls. After the early Cherokee, who shied from the area, the next people to venture into the gorge were the early European trappers who came into the mountains to deal in fur. In addition to trading with the Indians for pelts, these mountain men also did their own hunting. Once a year they would bring their goods down river to Augusta for the

"Gatherings." Companies out of Charleston, such as *Macartan and Campbell*, kept warehouses in Augusta and at Silver Bluff, a short way further down stream. Although the fur traders might spend most of the year in the mountains, occasionally marrying into the tribes, they did not hold land.

After the treaty of 1817-18, the Cherokee land became part of the United States. A land lottery followed, and the countryside was open to settlement. Tallulah

Gorge remained a wild, isolated area. The few who did move into the area were either hermits or very colorful characters, such as Adam Vandever (who was called Squire). Some of these people lived in isolation within the gorge itself, while others contented themselves by acting as early tour guides and entertaining the occasional visitor with tall tales.

Tallulah Falls - 1856
The First Tourists

Tallulah Falls - 1856
The First Tourists

Once the fear of the gorge as a place of mystery was overcome, newcomers to the area sought out the unusual creation of nature for its natural beauty. The nearest lodging for visitors was in Clarkesville. By the 1830s, this little village had become recognized as an ideal place for residents of the low country of Georgia and the Carolinas to escape the heat and yellow fever prevalent during the hot summer months. Hotels and rooming houses provided room and board. For entertainment, visitors could hire a rig from the livery stable behind the *Spencer House* on the Square and visit the scenic beauties in the surrounding hills. What evolved was "*The Grand Tour*" of the mountains. A spectacular stop in this ramble along the primitive roadways was a visit to the rim of Tallulah Gorge.

As visitors increased, the residents in the immediate area began to provide a few refreshments. They also developed a rough system of paths that descended into the chasm to better views of the cascades. Soon each waterfall had its own descriptive name: *Ladore, Tempesta, Hurricane, Oceana, Bridal Veil, Serpentine* and *Sweet Sixteen*. By 1882, when the railroad finally made its way to the area, the tourist boom was on.

Tallulah Falls - 1900 The Grand Era

Tallulah Falls - 1900 The Grand Era

The arrival of modern transportation in the form of the railroad opened the area around the rim of the gorge for all sorts of commercial ventures. There were many hotels and rooming houses built to accommodate the flood of visitors arriving daily from all over the country. The tourists of the early part of the century did not demand the variety of delights we are bombarded with today. Good food, comfortable rooms, fresh air, music for dancing, croquet and lawn tennis, and plenty of places to walk and explore exotic locations to stir the romantic Victorian imagination were enough to make Tallulah into the *"Niagara of the South."* Writers of fiction used the wild rustic setting for novels. Honeymoon couples flocked to the area for a memorable beginning to their new lives together. Excursion trains ran weekend specials from Atlanta for $3.35 round trip. The hotel band from the Cliff House, across the tracks from the station, met the arrivals with music on the platform.

The grand era lasted until several events changed the course of Tallulah's history. In the early decades of the 20th century, the river was dammed to provide hydroelectric power. This brought the waterfalls and their attraction to a standstill. Paved roads, automobiles, and the creation of a chain of lakes extending into the mountains gave travelers more options. With greater choices, the visitors demanded more than the simple pleasures which had satisfied earlier generations.

Happily, the bypassing of the area by the ravages of modern diversions has served to preserve this wonder of natural beauty. Its fauna and flora remain intact for the more discerning visitors to appreciate and preserve.

Detail

Cleveland - 1927

As I have mentioned, (over and over like a broken record!) the railroad was responsible for the beginning of many towns along its route. Cleveland was an exception. Long before the *Gainesville and Northwestern Railroad* was created in 1912 to transport lumber from the mill village of Helen, Cleveland had been not only a town but the county seat of White County. The county was created from part of Habersham in 1857 and named for Benjamin Cleveland. The historic red brick courthouse was commissioned in 1859 and completed during the Civil War.

The site for the train station was on part of the *Henderson Hotel* property. The hotel can be seen behind the station. The first depot was built in 1912. It was destroyed by fire two years later and in 1915, a second

building also burned. The final station, which is seen in the picture, was much larger than its predecessors.

After the establishment of regular service, the railroad became an important part of the town's development. Tom Hunt of Mountain View Community met the train daily with his two-mule team to deliver luggage to any location in town for 10¢. In 1922, A. L. Mauney Sr. arrived by train with his family and started the *Cleveland Grocery Company* located in the long low building across from the station. Summer traffic to Nacoochee Valley made good use of the railroad, as did local residents bound for Gainesville. After the big lumber company in Helen sold out in

1930, the train ceased operation. The tracks were removed in 1933.

But Cleveland did not fade away. It had been there before the railroad arrived. Its purpose as a center for community life was still important. Today Cleveland is still flourishing. It would be difficult to see any physical evidence of the brief time when this was a true "railroad town."

Cleveland - 1927

Logan Turnpike - 1920

Logan Turnpike - 1920

Turnpikes provided an early way of building roads of any length. As on any toll road, those using the passage were charged a fee. In addition, the investors might also have personal interests in the destination of the road for further profits. The *Unicoi Turnpike* had been chartered in 1813. A second turnpike was chartered in 1821 as the *Union Turnpike Company*. It traveled from Loudsville through Tesnatee Gap to Blairsville and on toward the Tellico Plains in Tennessee. The new road was 20 feet wide with 12 foot causeways. It was completed the same year it was chartered.

The main purpose of this road was to connect the mountain farmers with markets in Gainesville and to bring supplies over the gap to merchants in the isolated communities. The big difficulty with the road was the ascent and descent over Tesnatee Gap, which rose 3,138 feet above sea level. All hands were needed to push a heavy wagon on the way up. For the trip down, logs were tied to the rear of the vehicle to keep the team from being overrun by the load. Still, it was the main route and traffic was often quite heavy.

Monday was always the day for packing the wagons, as no respectable person worked on Sunday. Sometimes as many as thirty wagons would set out on Tuesday morning to make the two-day trip south. The return was usually on Saturday. Going to the market the wagons would be loaded with country hams, chestnuts, animal skins, sorghum syrup, chickens, chinquapins, ginseng, apples and eggs (packed in corn meal to avoid breakage). On the way back, the wagons carried hardware, dry goods, staples like coffee, sugar and tea, as well as other necessities unavailable in the hills.

A stagecoach also ran from Augusta, Georgia, over the mountains to Athens, Tennessee. Almost daily in good weather you might see drummers, cattlemen, lawmen and politicians along the road. On foot, drovers herded pigs, sheep and turkeys to market. Their roaming herds were often belled to keep track of strays. Even the turkeys wore tiny bells fashioned by the farm blacksmiths!

After the Civil War, Major Willis Logan bought extensive land on the south slope of the Blue Ridge Mountains in western White County. The land included 7½ miles of the turnpike road. Major Logan paid $3000 in 1871 for the rights to the toll road. It then came to be called the *Logan Turnpike*. It was also called *Tennessee Trail*, *The Tesnatee Turnpike*, the *Town Creek Road* and the *Drovers Road*. Major Logan's home was the stop for the stagecoach, as well as the place for paying fees, and became known as *Tollgate House*. Across the branch in a clearing, the farmers would often camp out near *Wagon Springs* on their way to market.

The fee to travel the road ranged from 2¢ per mile for four-wheel wagons with two or more horses or oxen, to one mil per mile for each head of sheep or pigs. Walkers and natives of Union, Lumpkin, White and Habersham Counties paid no fee. In 1917, the first automobile used the road. The experience was so traumatic that the driver took to her hotel bed on arriving in Blairsville!

The road continued in the same ownership until 1922. It was officially closed in 1925 when Highway 129 was opened. Tollgate House was torn down in 1939. Traces of the old road can still be followed on foot along its twisted journey over the gap.

Detail

Lumpkin Campground - 1930

In times gone by August meant *"lay-by time."* This was the time when the crops were reaching their maturity and folks laid down their tools to wait for the harvest. It was a brief period when there was leisure enough to think of other things. It was a time to get out your Sunday-go-to-meeting clothes, scrub the red clay off the children, and get ready for Camp Meeting. Wagons would be loaded with fresh vegetables, canned goods and watermelons, blankets and bedding, pots, pans, buckets and cooking utensils. Ahead lay a week of preaching, singing, and dinners on the grounds.

The site of camp meetings often reached back to the days of the early pioneers. At first, there might be only a *"brush arbor"* made of saplings, with pine boughs for a roof. Eventually, a permanent pavilion would be built, and in much later times, electricity and running water were added. Surrounding the arbor, a group of rough cabins would be built, although they would always be called *"tents."*

Long-standing traditions are still honored. The trees in the grove between the tents and the arbor were always painted with whitewash up about four feet from the base. In the days of kerosene lanterns, the reflection of the whitewash would help the congregation find their way to the evening service without bumping these obstacles. A conch shell, brought from the coast in 1910, is used at the Lumpkin Campground to call people to worship. Fresh hay is used to carpet the red clay floor of the arbor. Fans, traditionally provided by the local funeral parlor, are used to stir the heavy night air. Services are usually held three times a day, concluding with an evening of singing and preaching.

Although the days of small farming have all but disappeared, the camp meeting tradition is very much alive today. Some members of the congregation claim to have attended every year of their lives. It is a time for revival, not only of the spirit but of the feeling of community. The Lumpkin Campground dates back to 1830, while others scattered through the hills, at Mossy Creek, Loudsville and elsewhere, have an equally long history. So when the heat of August begins to bear down, you may be sure that in many communities the night air will be filled with sounds of *"In The Sweet By And By"* and *"God Be With You"* - and He still is.

Lumpkin Campground - 1930

Mt. Airy Presbyterian Church - 1920

Mt. Airy Presbyterian Church - 1920

At the height of Mt. Airy's time as a summer resort, Dr. S. L. Morris helped to organize the Mt. Airy Presbyterian Church in September, 1906. It was situated on the crest of the hill overlooking the train station and the *Monterey Hotel*, which had just been rebuilt following the fire of 1900. Times were good for the village, with as many as twenty trains passing through daily, bringing a flood of summer visitors from as far away as New Orleans. But by 1925, when the hotel again caught fire and burned to the ground, the impulse to rebuild was gone. The village began to fade except for a few residents who loved the area and kept their homes there.

The church survived until it was finally closed in 1978. In 1979, the building was given to the Cornelia Presbyterian Church. Today it is maintained by donations which provide for the physical needs of the building. The interior has been preserved along with the original wooden pews. The decorative kerosene lamps have been electrified, and the potbellied stove has been replaced with gas heat. An antique mahogany grand piano was given to the church in 1990. Overall, there is a timeless feeling of the past that lingers both inside and out. The church now serves as a chapel for weddings, Christmas Eve services, and other special events.

Winter on Burton

Winter on Burton

Winter in the mountains has a stillness that can cause city dwellers to wonder if they have suddenly gone deaf. But for those attuned to the area, there are still sounds that have meaning: the occasional wild bird call, a chain saw grinding in some distant wood lot, a dog announcing the approach of a stranger, or even the sound of a pickup truck laboring over a steep grade. These give evidence of life in an otherwise slumbering nature.

Lake Burton in winter is a landscape most summer visitors never see. The deep blue waters are lowered, leaving some coves reduced to only small stream beds that wander off looking for companionship. Occasionally even the former streets of the village of Burton at the bottom of the lake are visible to explore like the lost city of Atlantis. The docks stand like so many daddy-longlegs overlooking the mud flats that will disappear with the coming of spring rains. This is a time for construction and repair. Rock seawalls, new boat docks and pavilions appear.

But when the snow comes, this activity ceases. Snow muffles even the ears of the natives. It reduces our vision to a world wrapped in soft, fuzzy whiteness. Suddenly to take a step out the door is to walk into a strange new land. It is time to build up the fire and relax. Soon the magic will melt away. Our mountains are not a part of the world that stays locked in winter for long. A little sunshine breaking through the grey overhead will put us back in the business of getting ready for the summer season.

Snow is like the visitor who does not overstay his welcome – we are glad to see it come, and we are glad to see it go.

Detail from Mt. Airy - 1920

About Art and the Artist

I do not want to close without saying at least a word to those who often say to me, "*I wish I could do watercolor, but it is too hard*." Think again. The secret, if there is one, is not so much in learning how to do watercolors as it is how to let go of the doing.

In watercolor, you are not alone in the creative process. Your co-workers are the paper, the pigment, and the water. Each has certain rules of behavior. Better still, let me call them "*truths*" of behavior. When you paint in oil, the colors go where you put them. In watercolor, the water can move the pigment around– the pigments can react in strange and sometimes wonderful ways with each other – and the paper can receive or reject the combinations, depending on its own properties, the climate, and unknown forces that I am still amazed to discover.

The greatest control I have over a painting is in the beginning. I start with an idea and sketch it out on bits of paper – the composition, values and details. Once I move to the big sheet of white nothingness, I begin to relinquish my authority. I transfer the sketch to the surface in pencil, noting the white areas that must be saved if I want to take full advantage of the paper. Nothing is as white as the paper itself.

If there is a sky in the picture, then I begin there. For me, the sky happens in one attempt; if the sky fails, then I usually have to start over. I begin by selecting the colors that will capture the mood of the clouds, weather, and time of day I want to express. Then I wet the paper, roughly in the desired area, dip into the colors, and "*think sky*." As soon as I feel the work is heading in the right direction, I get out of the way and watch. If I continue to try and control the result at this point, it usually goes wrong. It's like baking a cake – if you keep opening the oven and sticking straws into it, the whole thing can go flat. In watercolor, the final effect can be seen only after the paper has dried. This explains why there is no answer to how long it takes to paint a picture. Part of the time the picture is painting itself. In the end, you either have God's sky or your own mess.

From there on, I paint generally from light to dark, loose to tight – watching the picture proceed with almost no conscious thought of which color or brush I am using. Artists have their own procedures. Some paint dark to light others light to dark. Some even paint top to bottom, bringing the scene down like a window shade. Some people think only in value tones while others are colorists. Some paint to express their inmost emotions. These persons often do not have to

Detail from Lakemont - 1927

know how to draw. For myself, I seek to tell a story and convey a feeling of mood, time, and light. Being an illustrator first, I also have perhaps too great a love for details and often *"over-ice my cake."* I readily admit to the fault of often *"running off at the paint brush."* However, if I am excessive in my details, I fall in the other category in choosing my colors. I use a very limited palette and mix most of my secondary colors (such as greens) in order to keep a family relationship in the results. If my colors were like a keyboard, my instrument would be a mandolin rather than a grand piano. Too many choices in color would keep me mentally on the surface of the painting rather than within it.

If all of this sounds too vague, then I suggest you explore the many fine books on teaching watercolor. There you will learn all of the basic tools and techniques that are at your disposal. In addition, many artists have their own special approaches that make their work individual. Take what appeals to you, stir it around in your own palette, and then express it in your own way. Combine what you *"know"* with what you *"feel."* Then get out of the way.

When I finally think I have finished a painting, I add three little birds somewhere in the sky. I call them my *"Trinity Birds."* It is my way of saying *"thanks"* to the One who is really doing my work – not *"by me,"* but *"through me."* Amen.

At this point, I do not know what direction this historic series will take next. I get many suggestions, in the post office, at the grocery store check-out and occasionally from the persons in the pew behind me at church. It is very rewarding to think that there is so much interest in having our past recreated. In this, I suppose my original purpose has been realized, since so many more people have become aware of the rich heritage they have around them. To have been part of this sharing has been an important part of my career. Some artists are artists only. I have always found that being part of people, history, and the miracles of nature each day is as much a part of my art as watching paint flow on paper. I thank God each day for the the opportunity to to continue sharing His world with others through the gifts He has given me.

I would like to acknowledge the ownership of the original art for the paintings used in this book, but over the years some of the paintings have changed hands, and I do not know for sure where they have come to rest. Rather than make mistakes or leave out some names, I have chosen to simply say that they have all been adopted, and I hope the families they are living with are finding them good company.

The prints included in this book were issued as follows:

Print	Year	Qty	Print	Year	Qty
On the Square, Clarkeville	1978	250	*Mt. Airy - 1920 (street and station)*	1992	500
Nora Mill	1984	150	*Currahee Mountain - 1873*	1993	500
Demorest - 1910	1985	250	*Sautee Store - 1934*	1993	1000
Nacoochee Valley Road - 1925	1985	250	*Baldwin - 1921*	1993	500
Cleveland - 1912	1986	250	*Sautee Valley Spring*	1993	1000
Cornelia - 1926	1986	350	*Autumn on Burton*	1993	500
Mt. Airy - 1915 (hotel)	1986	150	*Plowing Time*	1993	750
Sautee Creek Bridge -1905	1986	250	*Toccoa Falls - 1908*	1994	1000
Crescent Hill Church - 1936	1987	200	*Leaf - 1926*	1994	750
Grace Church - 1858	1987	300	*Watts Mill - 1930*	1994	1000
Rusharon	1987	200	*Battle of the Narrows - 1864*	1994	1000
Washington Street -1909	1987	450	*Mt. Airy School - 1938*	1994	500
Blue Creek Mill - 1925	1988	200	*Nacoochee - Prehistory (mound set)*	1995	1000
Dahlonega Baptist Church	1988	100	*Nacoochee - 1832 (mound set)*	1995	1000
Helen - 1920	1988	1000	*Nacoochee - 1923 (mound set)*	1995	1000
Rabun Home	1988	200	*Nacoochee - 1940 (mound set)*	1995	1000
Byron Herbert Reece Homeplace	1989	500	*Crossroads Store - 1935*	1995	1000
Glen-Ella Springs -1889	1989	200	*Bethlehem Baptist Church - 1930*	1995	1000
Mountain City - 1910 (RR set)	1989	500	*Blairsville - 1930*	1996	1000
Nacoochee School - 1943	1989	500	*Consolidated Gold Mine - 1904*	1996	1000
Clarkesville - 1912 (RR set)	1990	500	*Cleveland - 1927*	1996	1000
Demorest - 1900 (RR set)	1990	500	*Spring on Burton*	1996	1000
Auraria - 1834	1990	300	*Winter on Burton*	1996	1000
Lakemont - 1927 (RR set)	1990	500	*Lumpkin Campground - 1930*	1996	750
Nacoochee United Methodist Church	1990	200	*Mt Airy Presbyterian Church - 1920*	1997	1000
Tallulah Falls - 1905 (RR set)	1990	500	*Logan Turnpike - 1920*	1997	1000
Clarksville - 1912 (Square)	1991	1000	*Tallulah Falls - Land of Legends*	1997	1000
Clayton - 1938 (RR set)	1991	500	*Tallulah Falls 1820 - Hunters & Hermits*		
Cornelia - 1942 (RR set)	1991	500		1997	1000
			Tallulah Falls 1865 - The First Tourist		
Baptist Church Hill	1991	225		1997	1000
Main Street, Toccoa (early 1900s)	1991	450	*Tallulah Falls 1900 - The Grand Era*		
Turnerville- 1920 (RR set)	1991	500		1997	1000
Dahlonega - 1861 (Blue Ridge Rifles)	1992	500			